THE MISADVENTURES OF THE GALLOPING GOOSE

RETOLD BY PHILLIP NILSSON
ILLUSTRATED BY PATRICIA SINEX

The Misadventures of the Galloping Goose
All Rights Reserved.
Copyright © 2023 Phillip Nilsson
v3.0, r1.1

This is a work of fiction. The events and characters described herein are imaginary and are not intended to refer to specific places or living persons. The opinions expressed in this manuscript are solely the opinions of the author and do not represent the opinions or thoughts of the publisher. The author has represented and warranted full ownership and/or legal right to publish all the materials in this book.

This book may not be reproduced, transmitted, or stored in whole or in part by any means, including graphic, electronic, or mechanical without the express written consent of the publisher except in the case of brief quotations embodied in critical articles and reviews.

Outskirts Press, Inc.
http://www.outskirtspress.com

ISBN: 978-1-9772-5947-9

Illustrations by Patricia Sinex © 2023 Phillip Nilsson

Outskirts Press and the "OP" logo are trademarks belonging to Outskirts Press, Inc.

PRINTED IN THE UNITED STATES OF AMERICA

Dedicated
to children of all ages
who love trains
and true stories about them.

~~~~

Acknowledgements:
I would like to thank
the Colorado Railroad Museum in Golden Colorado
for their excellent library of source books
and their preservation of Galloping Geese #2, 6, and 7.
Special thanks to my loving wife, Dana,
who helped this idea become a reality.

This Book Belongs to:

_____

Once upon a time—sort of long ago, and kind of far away—there was a little railroad called The Rio Grande Southern. This narrow-gauge short line railroad carried people, mail, and freight over 161 miles of mountain passes, valleys, and steep cliffs in Southwestern Colorado.

The Rio Grande Southern mostly carried supplies to gold and silver mines. But it also carried mineral ores back from the mines to smelters in Durango and Denver. And, it carried sheep and cattle from ranches along the line as well as lumber cut from trees to build houses in the towns like Dolores, Telluride, Durango, Ophir and Ridgway. It even carried people going to work or to visit family.

During the 1930's when there were few jobs for people and not a lot of business for the railroad, Mr. Miller, the railroad manager, wanted to cut the costs of running the Railroad. He said to Jack, the master mechanic in Ridgway, "We need to run a train every day to move the passengers, the US mail, packages, and some freight items. But to run a large steam locomotive with an engineer, a fireman to shovel tons of coal and a brakeman in the caboose is just too expensive. We need to think of something else."

So, a somewhat feather-brained idea was hatched. Take an automobile for passengers, add a frame, and add flanged wheels and a box for freight, use a little gas instead of tons of coal and make the engineer a motorman! Yes! This should do it.

Master Mechanic Jack, with the help of the "back shop boys" at the Ridgway round house, got busy building something. They welded, sawed, nailed, cut, torched, riveted, sanded, machined, hammered, and painted…. some kind of thing!

The first "thing" was built with a Buick Master 6 automobile with added flanged wheels from a railroad car and a box built on the back of it, and then a cow catcher was added to the front to make it look like a train.

Even though the motor-powered thing looked funny, it worked well and was put to use right away moving passengers, mail and small freight items. The thing was originally called a "motor." The local people were not sure of what they saw. The wheels, not totally round, rolling on uneven rails, made the thing bounce and waddle down the track.

The engine covers from the automobile front, were left open to keep the engine from overheating. They flapped up and down with every bump and bounce on the track. The passengers, unsure of the newfangled thing flying over the track with a honking horn instead of a solid whistle of a steam locomotive, were flabbergasted. "Why look at that contraption, waddling and flapping and honking just like some kind of galloping goose!" Thus, it came to be called The Galloping Goose.

The Galloping Goose was so successful that six more were hatched. Similar to the original, but each different, they were built from 1920's era Pierce Arrow automobiles and spare railroad parts.

Although the gaggle of geese fleet was successful for the railroad, a few problems came home to roost. Sometimes there were animals on the tracks.

On another occasion, the railroad got into trouble with the US Postal Inspector when a US mailbag and some mail was singed from getting too close to the wood stove which was in the passenger compartment to keep the passengers warm. The mail inspector also became worried that passengers would start reading the mail.

Sometimes, rocks blocked the train tracks!

One day there was serious trouble, a Goose and its passengers were leaving the snow shed at the top of Lizard Head Pass when the Galloping Goose's drive shaft broke, which also broke the line to the brakes.

The Galloping Goose started to fly down the pass faster and faster toward Trout Lake. Motorman Fred was unable to slow the flapping Goose. He had to think fast. What could he do to save the passengers?

So, Fred told the passengers to fly the coop. They flew safely out of the fast-moving Goose into snow banks.

Then Fred himself flew off the Goose which was now on the loose and flying very fast down the tracks with nobody to fly it!

Motorman Fred ran to the nearest telephone along the rail line and called the Station Agent at Ophir.

"A Goose has flown the coop and if it doesn't fly off the track, it will be flying your way really soon!"

The Station Agent called the track workers at Vance Junction as the Galloping Goose flew past her station.

"There's a runaway Goose on the loose! Try to catch it!"

The track workers grabbed a nearby large chain and threw it across the rails, and a little further down they threw a second chain across the rails. After all, if one is good, two are better.

The workers then waited a safe distance away to see what would happen. Would the chains stop the Goose? Would this wild Goose chase be over?

The flying Goose hit the first chain crashing and banging over the chain but not stopping. The first chain just slowed the runaway Goose.

The second chain was dragged along the track by the wheels of the Goose and with a loud and long screech, the Goose finally rattled and groaned to a stop. Yes, the wild Goose chase was finally over! The passengers had a long walk to the station with their feathers a little ruffled, but otherwise unharmed. The Galloping Goose was up and waddling, and flapping and honking on the tracks the very next day.

Despite all the feathery troubles, the fleet of Galloping Geese kept the Rio Grande Southern Railroad in business for many more years.

So it could be said, that the Galloping Goose was the golden egg that saved The Rio Grande Southern Railroad!

Glossary

<u>Back Shop Boys</u>: Shop workers who built and repaired the Geese fleet.

<u>Brakeman</u>: Person who rode in the caboose and made sure the brakes worked.

<u>Business</u>: What you need to mind and how the Rio Grande Southern made money.

<u>Consist</u>: The complete train with locomotive, cars and caboose.

<u>Cow Catcher</u>: The part in front of locomotives and Galloping Geese used to push obstacles off the tracks.

<u>Drive Shaft</u>: rotating shaft that transfers power from the Goose motor to the wheels.

<u>Engineer</u>: The person who drives the train.

<u>Fireman</u>: The person who shoveled coal into the locomotive and maintained the steam pressure.

<u>Flanged</u>: A rim on a metal wheel to maintain position on the rails.

<u>Master Mechanic</u>: The person who designed all the Galloping Geese, also in charge of locomotive and train car repairs.

<u>Motorman</u>: Galloping Goose engineer/fireman/brakeman. (Also known as Motormouth, telling stories to passengers)

<u>Narrow Gauge</u>: Railroad Rails placed 36 inches apart compared to Standard gauge which is 4 feet and 8.5 inches apart.

<u>Ophir</u>: (sounds like gopher) A Station along the Rio Grande Southern Railroad.

<u>Riveted</u>: Using small metal fasteners heated by a torch to hold metal parts together by hammering.

<u>Round House</u>: Semicircular building with multiple stalls to store and repair locomotives, also known as a Galloping Goose Coop.

<u>Station Agent</u>: Sold tickets to passengers and generally ran the station.

<u>Short Line</u>: A small Railroad serving a local area.

<u>Torched</u>: Using a gas torch to cut metal and to weld metal pieces together.

You can visit a Galloping Goose. Goose #1 has been rehatched, (replicated) and is at the Ridgway Railroad Museum in Ridgway, Colorado. Geese #'s 2, 6, and 7 are roosting at The Colorado Railroad Museum in Golden, Colorado. Goose #3 is at Knotts Berry Farm in California. Goose #4 is in Telluride, Colorado and Goose #5 is in Dolores, Colorado.

About the Author

I have been a train enthusiast almost all my life. I also love history and geology. Living in Durango, CO with my wife, three children and a dog is the perfect place to enjoy all of these things together. Colorado has a rich and colorful history and I wrote this book to share these interests with children to encourage curiosity about the people and history of Colorado.

—Phillip Nilsson

The author, Phillip Nilsson, with his dog Rio,
(short for Rio Grande Southern)
on a 1/5 scale model of Goose #6.

About the Illustrator

I was born with a sense of joy and fascination in color and form. Along the way, people and places have been my inspiration. These factors influenced me in everything I saw and did. I hope as you read this book, it brings to you, the pleasure it gave me in creating it.

—Patricia Sinex

Printed in the USA
CPSIA information can be obtained
at www.ICGtesting.com
JSHW040427190324
59346JS00001B/2